30117    0130176

WITHDRAWN FROM STOCK
OFFERED FOR SALE
WITH ANY FAULTS BY
CITY OF WESTMINSTER LIBRARIES

PRICE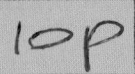

WESTMINSTER CITY LIBRARIES
PIMLICO LIBRARY
RAMPAYNE STREET
LONDON SW1V 2

### ANIMALS ARE AMAZING!

# mini-beasts

# DAVID TAYLOR

BOXTREE

First published in Great Britain in 1990 by Boxtree Limited
Copyright © Boxtree Limited 1990
Front cover illustration and all artwork by David Quinn

Designed by Bet Ayer
Senior Editor Cheryl Brown
Edited by Heather Dewhurst
Typeset by York House Typographic
Printed in Singapore
For Boxtree Limited,
36 Tavistock Street,
London WC2E 7PB

**British Library Cataloguing in Publication Data**
Taylor, David, *1934-*
  Mini-beasts.
  1. Arthropoda
  I. Title    II. Series
  595.2

ISBN 1-85283-316-5

# CONTENTS

World of the mini-beasts — 10

Bee — 12

Spider — 14

Woodlouse — 16

Frog — 18

Ladybird — 19

Mite — 20

Scorpion — 21

Snail — 22

Centipede and millipede — 23

Flea — 24

Ant — 26

Bombardier beetle — 27

Amazing facts! — 28

Imagine that one day I give you a drink from my magic bottle. All of a sudden you find yourself getting smaller and smaller until your friendly cat seems as big as an elephant, and

the chair you are sitting on looks like a mountain! Now you are small enough to explore the strange world of the mini-beasts!

The bee is a very busy creature. It buzzes around the garden, taking pollen from one flower to another and feeding on nectar, a sweet food made in flowers. The bee makes honey in its hive.

Sometimes you might see lots of bees flying together in a swarm or big group. They can be very dangerous. Once a swarm of killer bees attacked a town in South America and firemen had to fight them with flame throwers!

The spider spins a web from silk made in its body and uses the web to catch flies and other insects. Some spiders live in the house. You might even see one in the bath!

Some spiders are very dangerous to other animals. The black widow spider is poisonous and can kill a mouse with just one bite!

The woodlouse looks like a small army tank! It likes to live in a damp, shady place and feed on rotting plant food and soft green leaves.

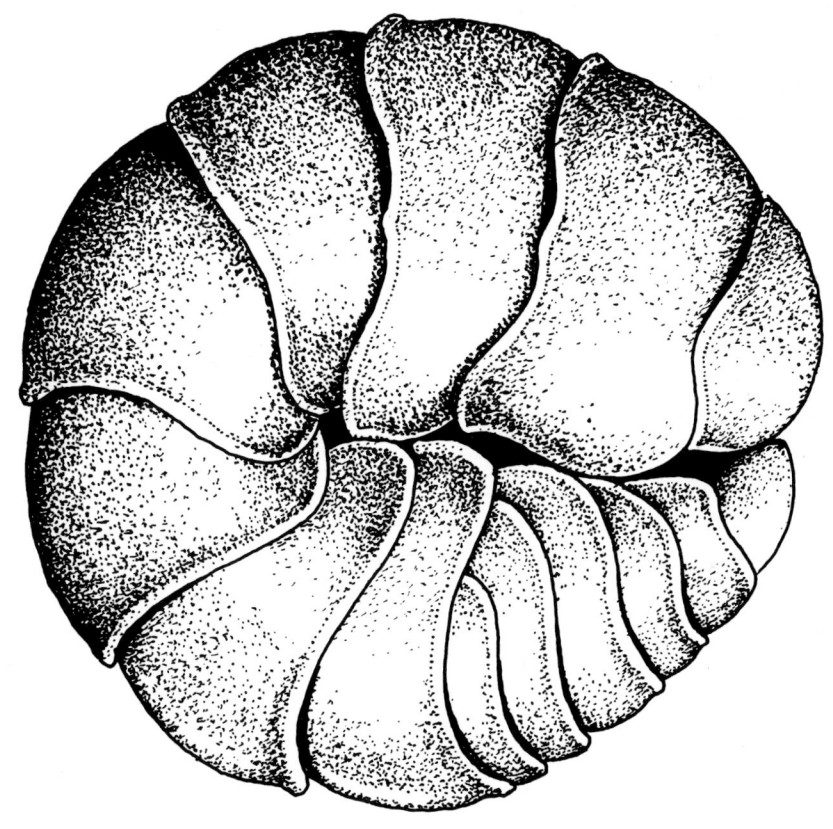

The woodlouse is a very shy creature. As soon as it hears anyone coming, it curls up in a ball to hide.

Frogs live in ponds but they also like to hop on the ground. They have strong back legs and are very good at jumping.

The ladybird is a pretty insect. To take a closer look, pick one up very gently and it will crawl over your hand. Ladybirds can also fly very well.

Mites are so small that you can only see them through a magnifying glass. They live all over the world, in the sea, on the land, in the dust in your house and even in animals.

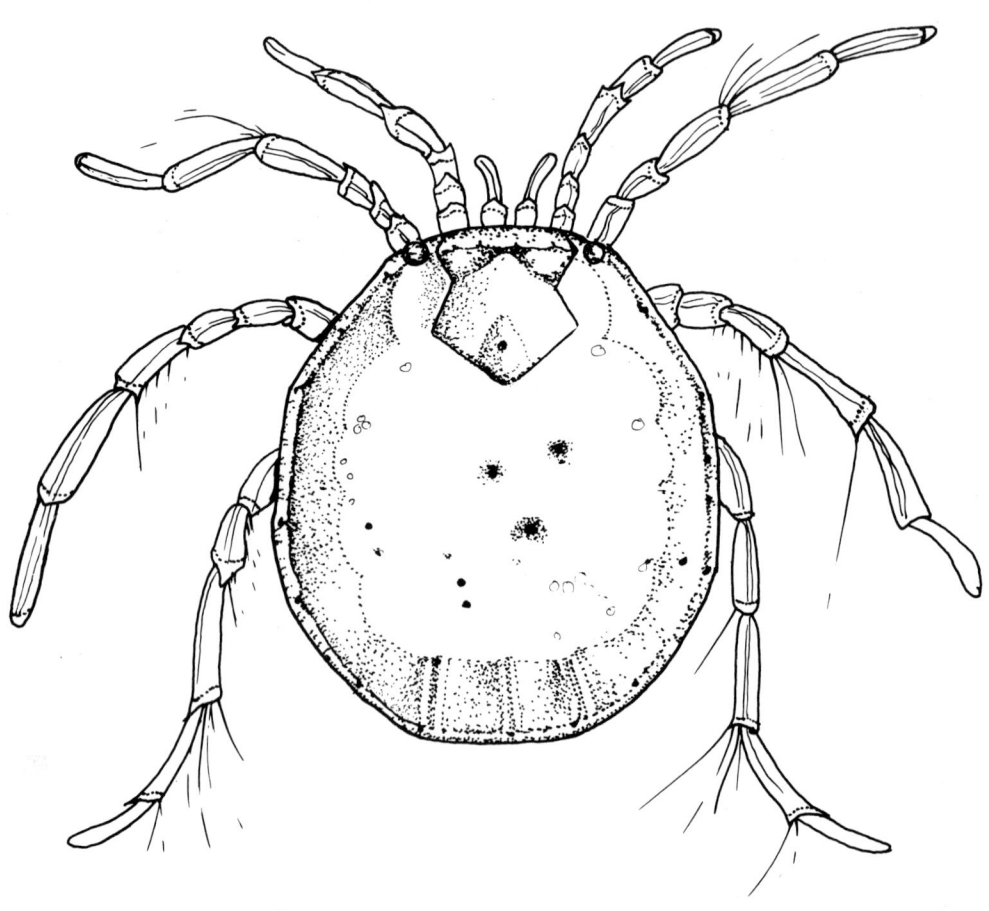

The scorpion is a bigger cousin of the mite. It lives in hot places. When the scorpion is hungry, it catches an insect with its front claws and then stings it with its tail.

The snail has a shell on its back. When the snail is tired or wants to hide, it curls up inside the shell. The thrush likes to eat snails. It cracks open the shell on a stone and then eats the snail's body.

Centipedes have lots of legs and millipedes have even more! They both live in the soil in the garden. Centipedes feed on insects but millipedes only eat plant food.

The flea is a very small animal that can jump very high – up to 130 times its own height. This would be the same as a man jumping up to the top of the Eiffel Tower in Paris!

When I was a boy I was fascinated by the 'flea circus' at the local zoo. We watched the fleas through a magnifying glass. They walked on tightropes of fine hairs, 'fenced' with swords made of thin wire, and pulled tiny carriages.

Ants live in a nest with lots of other ants. They work well with each other and are always very busy. Ants are also clever creatures. They can find their way by looking at the sun and can also learn and remember things.

There are lots of different sorts of beetle. The bombardier beetle lives in hot places and has a special way of defending itself. If an ant tries to attack it from behind, the bombardier beetle shoots it with a poisonous spray.

# AMAZING FACTS!

1 There are lots more spiders in the world than people — in every acre of countryside there are about 2.5 million spiders!

2 The shell of the woodlouse is made mostly from chalk!

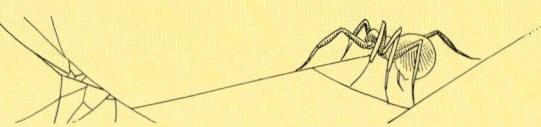

3 One type of mite, which is usually harmless, lives in the hair roots of human eyelashes!

4 Some ants are keen gardeners — they grow their own mushroom gardens!

5  Bees can 'talk' to each other by dancing! Other bees watch the dance and get the message at once.

6  The longest jumping frog is the sharp-nosed frog from South Africa – it can jump 10 metres in three leaps!

7  Fleas can last for a year without eating anything!

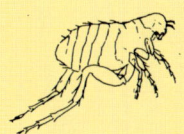

8  The biggest snail in the world is the giant African snail which can grow to 20 cms long. One of these snails can have about 11 million baby snails in five years!